GOLDEN MILLER BUSES INCLUDING CARDIFF BLUEBIRD

Philip Wallis

AMBERLEY

Acknowledgements

Inspiration for this book came from viewing Golden Miller photo collections of my friends Tony Wright, who worked in Feltham for many years, and Michael Dryhurst, whose 'stomping ground' was in north Surrey. Other photographers kindly searched their collections to allow a representative pictorial display of the varied routes, buses and coaches covered in this work, for which I am most grateful.

Stephen Telling, founder of Telling's Coaches and Managing Director of Tellings-Golden Miller, and Peter Bradley, formerly of London Regional Transport, gave valued help with research for this book. Other input was received from Dave Bubier, Laurie James, Chris Martin and Mark Worley.

Philip Wallis, Hawkchurch, Devon, August 2019

First published 2019

Amberley Publishing
The Hill, Stroud
Gloucestershire, GL5 4EP

www.amberley-books.com

Copyright © Philip Wallis, 2019

The right of Philip Wallis to be identified as the Author of this work has been asserted in accordance with the Copyright, Designs and Patents Act 1988.

ISBN 978 1 4456 9579 2 (print)
ISBN 978 1 4456 9580 8 (ebook)

British Library Cataloguing in Publication Data. A catalogue record for this book is available from the British Library.

Origination by Amberley Publishing.
Printed in the UK.

It was rare for other operators to run bus services entirely within London Transport's area. The 1933 London Passenger Transport Act gave London Transport (LT) monopoly status for bus service operation within a designated Special Area covering an approximate 25-mile radius from Charing Cross. A provision in the Act allowed LT to give consent to other operators to provide services in the Special Area. In practice, LT chose to operate almost all bus services within the Special Area itself, so few consents were granted.

London Transport came under the control of the Greater London Council (GLC) from 1 January 1970 when its responsibility became restricted to bus services within the 600 square mile GLC area. LT continued to hold power of veto over other operators' services entirely within the GLC area – the nomenclature changed from consent to agreement.

In the early 1950s LT had experienced reduced patronage, declining traffic receipts and a perception that its standards of operation were slipping. A Committee of Enquiry was appointed to investigate many facets of LT's road and rail operations. The Chambers Report, published in January 1955, contained its findings and recommended, in respect of unremunerative bus services, that: 'consideration should be given to allowing or even encouraging private operators to undertake minor services where London Transport cannot provide the services except at a substantial loss'. This led to a small number of independent operators obtaining LT consents over subsequent years. Golden Miller was one such operator.

Formation of Golden Miller

Golden Miller originated as a Twickenham coach operator established by Fred Varney in the 1930s. Reputedly Varney founded his business using a share of winnings he had been given after his father won the Irish Sweepstake with a stake on racehorse Golden Miller, a renowned champion that remains the only horse to have won both the Cheltenham Gold Cup and the Grand National in the same year – 1934. In recognition of the source of his good fortune, Varney named his business Golden Miller and traded as a small coach operator undertaking private hire and contract work.

Separately, in 1923 Frederick George Wilder, who had worked for a firm of furniture removers, started a road haulage business with compensation money paid to him after being crushed between two vehicles. His haulage business expanded after the Second World War but almost collapsed in the early 1950s as a consequence of the bankruptcy of its main client. Shaken by events, Leslie Wilder, Frederick's son, sought to diversify the business and bought a Bedford OB coach in 1955. Expansion followed that same year when F. G. Wilder & Sons of No. 61 Fern Grove, Feltham, purchased Fred Varney's Golden Miller Coaches, adopted Golden Miller as its trading name and based all activities at Feltham.

Leslie's wife Sylvia joined the firm and a decision was made in 1958 to concentrate on coach work with the bulk of the lorry fleet being sold. The following year saw the business relocate from rented premises to a freehold garage on the opposite side of Fern Grove. A limited liability company was formed on 10 April 1961. F. G. Wilder & Sons Ltd, trading as Golden Miller Coaches, went on to build a reputation for high-class private hire and became entirely a coaching business in 1966 when three remaining lorries were sold.

Into Bus Route Operation

Golden Miller Services (GM) entered into bus route operation on 20 January 1967 through its acquisition of Tourist Coachways of Hounslow. Tourist Coachways had been formed by Mr G. T. Mash to absorb the operations of West London Coachways Ltd upon the dissolution of that firm by Mr Mash and Mr T. V. Poulton. West London Coachways had inaugurated the first post-Chambers Report independently operated bus service within London Transport's Special Area on 1 September 1955 with a Bedfont to Feltham station route. Operation passed to Tourist Coachways on 1 January 1962.

Leslie Wilder quickly realised that the Bedfont bus service was barely breaking even. As acquired, it was two-person operated (driver and conductor) with service running into the late evening. After three months, one-man operation was implemented and evening journeys deleted. The service could then be worked by one driver on a spread-over shift with a midday relief driver. This saved two and a half shifts per day and the route became highly profitable.

Encouraged by the transformation of its Bedfont service, Golden Miller sought other bus route opportunities. Feltham was a commuting and shopping centre, with a frequent train service to Waterloo and the presence of major stores such as Sainsbury's and Tesco. In pursuing his expansionist aim, Leslie Wilder was advised by well-known industry figure John Fielder, Advertising Manager of *Coaching Journal*. Fielder had a broad interest in local bus operations and alerted operators to possible opportunities. He had learnt that demand existed for a bus service along the Elmwood Avenue area of Feltham and recommended a service between Feltham and Hanworth. Simultaneously parish councillors had approached Golden Miller about providing a service to the bus-less village of Charlton and, although John Fielder counselled against it, Leslie Wilder pressed ahead. Discussions ensued between Golden Miller and London Transport with the outcome that LT granted consent for GM to introduce two new bus routes, from Feltham station to Shepperton via Charlton and from Feltham station to Hanworth.

London Transport agreed a route numbering sequence for Golden Miller routes, ascending numerically from 601. This came into effect from 1 February 1968 with newly introduced services to Shepperton and Hanworth numbered 602 and 603 respectively and the Bedfont route numbered 601. Schedules were arranged such that the 602 and 603 could each be worked by one driver with one bus with gaps in service around midday for drivers' breaks. Three buses were needed to cover the 601, 602 and 603.

Ministry of Transport-approved bus stops were erected along those sections of GM routes (the majority) not served by LT. Flat fares of (old) sixpence applied to routes 601 and 603 with graduated fares on the 602. Buses were equipped with company-made Fareboxes into which passengers paid fares in sight of the driver. No tickets were issued.

Golden Miller's Plaxton-bodied Bristol LH6L CJJ 44H was photographed approaching route 601's Feltham terminus north of the railway station in March 1970. At this period the 601 ran every twenty minutes to Bedfont Green. (Philip Wallis)

The 601 was re-routed away from its Northumberland Crescent terminus at Bedfont to form a loop terminal working at Bedfont Green from 13 January 1969. A little earlier, the 601's terminus north of Feltham station had been relocated from east to west side of Bedfont Lane where a turning bay had been constructed.

Bedfont route 601 and Hanworth route 603 remained within London Transport's area of responsibility when it passed to GLC control on 1 January 1970. The bulk of Shepperton route 602 operated in Surrey with only its section between Feltham and Lower Feltham remaining in the GLC area.

The long-established Walton-on-Thames station service, in Surrey, was formally taken over from Walton Lodge Garage on 19 November 1970 and numbered 604. That route's town terminus at Walton Bridge was not far from the 602's terminus at Shepperton station and thought was given towards integrating the two routes, but the idea did not reach fruition. Around this time consideration was given to a new route in the Claygate area but, because of the likelihood of passenger carrying restrictions being imposed by LT, the concept of what might have become route 605 was not pursued.

John Fielder alerted Leslie Wilder to a further route opportunity in north Surrey. London Transport routes 203/203A (Twickenham–Staines/Ashford) did not serve certain new housing developments in Stanwell and West Bedfont. London Country route 444 only ran four Wednesday and Saturday journeys between Staines and Stanwell Moor, which Fielder considered not to meet demand. Lengthy discussions ensued, which led to the introduction of Staines to Stanwell Moor route 606 on 1 November 1971. GM's weekdays run-out increased to five buses – one on each of routes 601, 602, 603, 604 and 606.

Road construction projects hampered GM's activities at times. One day route 606's driver heading towards Staines found that the right-hand turn off Long Lane into London Road had been blocked. The only solution was to turn left and travel eastwards for around ¼ mile before finding a gap in the central reservation and making a U-turn – not the safest manoeuvre on the A30 trunk road. Wilder pursued the matter with the highway authority only to be told that it was not obliged to give him advance notice of blockages! Construction of the M3 motorway, with its link to the M4, necessitated temporary diversions to routes 602 and 603 in 1973/74, thus disrupting schedules. Wilder felt frustrated that road planners often failed to liaise with him – only LT's intervention ensured that he was included at some meetings.

Golden Miller had largely relied upon cheaper second-hand bus purchases to maintain its network. A change in vehicle policy was evident in September 1974 when three new Bedford YRQ buses, SYO 600–602N, joined the fleet. The Ministry of Transport had introduced a Bus Grant towards the purchase of new vehicles in September 1968 and increased the grant from 25 per cent to 50 per cent of the purchase price in November 1971. This tilted economics in favour of new vehicles.

Walton station service 604 had been extended to Oatland Village from 7 December 1970 in an effort to boost revenue. The peak-flow nature of this service made economic operation difficult and GM withdrew from it after 24 December 1974. The 604 was then operated by Mole Valley as a peak hour service until abandoned in June 1975.

A proposed extension of Bedfont Green route 601 along Hatton Road to the developing area of Hatton Cross, where it would have connected with the Underground's 1975 Piccadilly Line extension, was discussed with LT but never implemented.

Route number 605 finally came into use with the introduction of a schools service between Stanwell Moor and Stanwell on 6 September 1976. Run-out on school days was now five buses – one on each of routes 601, 602, 603, 605 and 606.

Tellings-Golden Miller

Telling's Coaches of Byfleet had been founded by Stephen and Christine Telling in 1972. That business grew steadily and, seeking further expansion, bought F. G. Wilder & Sons Ltd in December 1984 when Stephen Telling became Managing Director of Golden Miller.

Stephen Telling quickly reviewed the bus operation and realised that substantial changes needed to be made to ensure viability. He found that the bus fleet that he had purchased was not in particularly good mechanical order. In a bold move, GM's entire bus fleet – Bristol LH6L CJJ 44H, Bedford YRQs SYO 600–602N, Bedford YMT ELA 389T and AEC Swifts MBO 519F and SRS 50K – was sold to dealer Ensign in 1985. Peter Newman of Ensign supplied five Eastern Coach Works-bodied Bristol RELL6Gs – NLJ 827G, FVX 615H, POD 826H, TUO 255J and LNN 93K – as fleet replacements. Although the average age of this intake was 15 years, the buses were in sound mechanical order, having originated in National Bus Company subsidiaries fleets with good maintenance regimes.

Routes 602 and 605 were subsidised by Surrey County Council, with combined support of £10,000 in 1984. Stephen Telling was still dissatisfied with the financial performance of both routes and indicated to SCC his wish to withdraw them. Stanwell Schools route 605 last operated on 4 April 1985 and Feltham to Shepperton route 602 was reduced to Monday to Friday peak hour-only operation from 8 April 1985.

The trading title Tellings-Golden Miller (TGM) was adopted in June 1985. The business operated from two bases, at Byfleet and Feltham, which caused problems with control of operations and staff. Use of the Fern Grove premises in Feltham ceased in August 1985 when all TGM operations became based at Wintersells Road in Byfleet, although this increased 'dead mileage' for buses running to and from service.

Margaret Thatcher's Conservative government clashed with the left-wing policies of Labour-controlled GLC under Ken Livingstone. This ultimately led to the abolition of the GLC, during which process London Transport was put under government control from 29 June 1984. A competitive bus route tendering regime was introduced under which both commercial operators and London Buses' subsidiary companies could bid for route contracts with the first tranche implemented on 13 July 1985. Stephen Telling learnt from London Regional Transport's (LRT) Road Service Licencing Committee – which met fortnightly to consider applications from what it dubbed 'foreign operators' – that LRT's new bus route tendering regime would include TGM's Feltham area routes at some stage. Due consideration led Stephen Telling to sell Bedfont route 601 and Hanworth route 603 to Fountain Luxury Coaches with effect 22 October 1985.

Tellings-Golden Miller's Caetano-bodied Volvo B10M C89 NNV was on route 606's stand in Staines bus station on 16 May 1992. 'Stagecoach' wording on its front panel was branding for Caetano's body design, not a reference to the bus-operating mega-group based in Perth! (Mike Harris)

TGM continued to operate Shepperton route 602 and Staines to Stanwell Moor route 606 and purchased two Caetano-bodied Volvo B10M buses – C89 NNV and C188 RVV – to work them. Telling had hoped that additional off-peak Surrey CC tendered work would become available to occupy the bus which worked peak hours-only 602 but this did not materialise, so C188 RVV was sold. TGM passed operation of the 602 to Fountain in mid-1986 although the service registration was not transferred until 14 March 1988. This left TGM with just route 606.

Fountain Luxury Coaches Ltd

Fountain Luxury Coaches of Twickenham had been started by Alf Susan, renowned for driving in bedroom slippers! Separately, Isleworth Coaches had been formed by husband and wife Dennis and Doreen Blackford.

Isleworth Coaches' first foray into bus route operation arose as a consequence of industrial action in 1966 when LT Central Area crews imposed a ban on working voluntary overtime and rest days. LT temporarily withdrew services over certain sections of routes and gave consent to other operators to run replacements. Isleworth Coaches took up operation of Richmond to Richmond Hill route 235 on 31 January 1966. The dispute was soon settled and LT had restored its own buses to most routes by 19 March 1966. Exceptionally, LT did not resume service over route 235, which continued to be covered by Isleworth Coaches until operation passed to Continental Pioneer from 8 May 1968.

The Blackford's had acquired Fountain Luxury Coaches by 1977 and ran that business alongside Isleworth Coaches.

Fountain took up operation of Feltham to Bedfont Green route 601 and Feltham to Hanworth route 603 from 22 October 1985. Existing timetables were maintained using a mix of TGM's Bristol REs and coaches from Fountain's own fleet. Fountain moved its vehicles into the former TGM premises at Fern Grove, Feltham, in early 1986. By March 1986 Fountain had acquired former Trimdon Motor Services Leyland Leopard HUP 131N and use of TGM's Bristol REs declined.

Fountain combined routes 601 and 603 on 9 June 1986 to form new twenty-five-minute frequency route 600 between Bedfont Green and Hanworth via Feltham. The 600 ran entirely within London Regional Transport's area, so Fountain needed LRT's agreement to operate. This was forthcoming with the stipulation that LRT's outer-zone flat fare of 30p be applied, thus Fountain had no discretion to vary fares. Operation of route 600 did not go smoothly. Linking the two former routes meant that the 600 had to traverse Feltham level crossing in Bedfont Lane. The frequent railway service emanating from London's Waterloo station meant that the crossing gates were often closed, so delaying route 600 buses. Missing journeys attracted hostile press comment and led to frustrated passengers organising a protest petition submitted to the London Borough of Hounslow in 1988. The company admitted its difficulties, blaming a shortage of drivers and breakdowns.

Hounslow was keen on increasing operation of wheelchair-accessible buses after the success of route H20 (Hounslow–Ivybridge Estate), which was introduced in March 1989. Discussions ensued between Hounslow and LRT, represented by Mike Weston and Peter Bradley, about splitting the 600 into two extended services: H24 Feltham station–Hatton Cross via Bedfont Green and H25 Butts Farm Estate, Hanworth–Sparrow Farm Estate, Feltham. Fountain was brought into the discussions in March 1990 with the concept that Fountain would operate the H24 and that the H25 would be tendered. Fountain agreed to consider the proposal but events swiftly overtook such a plan. Fountain went into terminal decline and folded on Friday 6 April 1990.

Evolution of Route 600 into H24 and H25

LRT arranged for London Buses' subsidiary Westlink to work route 600 on a temporary contract from 7 April 1990. A tender process for replacement routes H24 and H25 was initiated with an outcome that both routes were awarded to London Buses' subsidiary London United from

29 September 1990. After a short delay, both routes became worked by wheelchair-accessible Iveco 49.10s with financial support from Hounslow. The service pattern was revised from 28 August 1993 when the H25 became a cross-Feltham service between Butts Farm Estate and Hatton Cross and the H24 was replaced by new route H26 (Sparrow Farm Estate–Hatton Cross via Lower Feltham).

Route H25, direct successor to Golden Miller routes 601 and 603, continues to run as a successful Transport for London bus route.

Drawlane Group

Tellings-Golden Miller was sold to holding company Drawlane in 1990, the acquisition being channelled through Drawlane subsidiary Midland Fox.

TGM started commuter operation with a Woking area to London service launched on 1 February 1990, which lasted around two years. TGM superseded London & Country as operator of Guildford area to London peak hour service 740 from 15 February 1992 and maintained that service until 27 October 2000.

LRT contracts for routes 116 (Brentford–Bedfont Green) and 117 (Brentford–Staines) were awarded from 10 August 1991 and operated by TGM Buses. An assortment of elderly Leyland Nationals, many from Midland Fox, was drafted in and based at the Speedlink garage in Staines. Unfortunately TGM Buses did not operate this contract with distinction. The refurbished Nationals could not cope with intensive London service and breakdowns occurred with resultant service unreliability. LRT soon lost patience and passed control of the routes to London & Country (another Drawlane subsidiary) on 1 January 1992, pending formal contract reassignment on 23 February 1992.

Drawlane became British Bus PLC on 14 December 1992. British Bus considered that coach-centric Tellings-Golden Miller did not fit its portfolio and sold TGM back to Stephen Telling in July 1993.

Cardiff Bluebird

Tellings-Golden Miller gained a foothold in Cardiff with the acquisition of coach operator Globeheath Ltd, trading as Coach Travel Centre, in April 1991, with premises at No. 307 Penarth Road, Grangetown.

TGM, trading as Cardiff Bluebird (CB), started Cardiff bus operation on 20 September 1993. Initial service was fifteen-minute-frequency Monday to Saturday daytime route 218 between central Cardiff and the suburb of Ely, which ran in direct competition with municipally-owned Cardiff Bus (Bws Caerdydd). CB's fares were cheaper than the municipal operator's and drivers gave change, whereas Cardiff Bus had an exact fare policy. Stephen Telling considered that the coaching ethos of his business, with emphasis on customer service, filtered through into his bus operations and made CB's services more welcoming. Route numbers were selected to give a form of numerical affinity with the principal Cardiff Bus service with which CB competed along any particular route corridor (thus: Cardiff Bus 18, Cardiff Bluebird 218 to Ely). Wood Street, near Cardiff bus station, was the city centre convergence point for CB's routes.

The company name was changed to Cardiff Bluebird Ltd in January 1995. Expansion followed, including tendered services around Bridgend. Many city routes were combined from mid-1995 to form cross-Cardiff services and progressively renumbered into a 200–209 block. Operations in January 1996 comprised routes 200–202 (Ely–St Mellons), 203–204 (Wood Street–Llanishen) 205–206 (Pentrebane–Llanrumney) and 207–209 (Ely–Pentwyn), whilst tendered route L3 ran between Ely and Llandough Hospital.

The fleet was largely second-hand with extremes of size – either large capacity double-deckers or mini/midibuses. Two new Plaxton Pointer-bodied Dennis Darts joined in 1995.

Increasing cost of diesel fuel was cited as one reason for closing down CB's operations after 7 September 1996.

Cardiff Bluebird's Northern Counties-bodied Leyland Atlanten 65 originated with Greater Manchester. It was seen in Kingsway working route 265 from St Mellons with Cardiff Bus' East Lancashire-bodied Leyland Olympian 517 in pursuit. (Philip Wallis)

The Last Original Golden Miller Services Bus Route

Staines to Stanwell Moor route 606 was extended across Staines Bridge to terminate at a new Sainsbury's superstore from 13 July 1992. TGM continued to operate the 606, using Volvo B10M C89 NNV, until 4 March 1995. The 606 was operated by London & Country between 6 March 1995 and 25 July 1997, after which it was incorporated into L&C route 436 (Englefield Green–Heathrow Airport).

Start of Exponential Expansion for Tellings-Golden Miller

TGM was awarded LRT's contract for route S3 (Belmont–Sutton–Worcester Park) from 8 April 1995. TGM took up Surrey CC's contract for route 513 (Kingston–Downside) on 2 September 1995 when it replaced London & Country. Further Surrey CC route contracts followed in 1997 and the LRT contract for route 235 (Brentford–Sunbury Village) was awarded from 10 January 1998. Under Stephen Tellings' leadership, Tellings-Golden Miller had entered an expansionist phase, which would see its operations grow in London and elsewhere in the country, its sale to the Arriva group in 2007 and its buy-back into Telling family ownership in 2016. This period warrants its own future account.

Golden Miller, Tellings-Golden Miller and Fountain Coaches Bus Routes in Feltham and Staines Areas 1967 – 1995

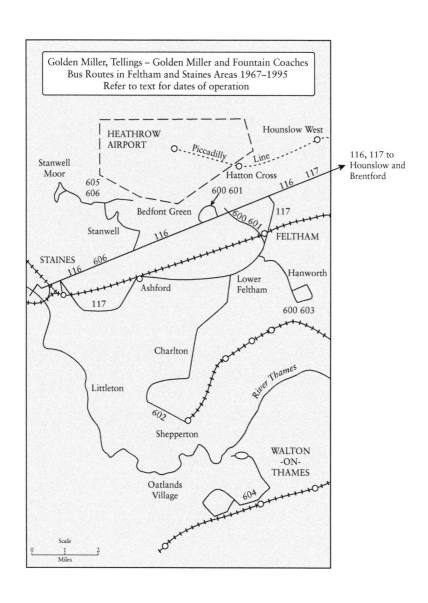

Route 601 Feltham Station–Bedfont (Bedfont Green from 13 January 1969)

West London Coachways 1948 Mulliner-bodied Bedford OB JXH 634 had left the bus terminus at Feltham station shortly after introduction of the Bedfont service in 1955. This bus originated in British Overseas Airways Corporation's fleet. (C. Carter, Author's collection)

Tourist Coachways habitually employed coaches on the Bedfont route. 1953 Duple-bodied Bedford SB OUO 587 was seen at the Feltham station terminus on 18 April 1964. (Roy Marshall, Author's collection)

A dedicated 'Omnibus Terminal' for the Bedfont route was constructed at Feltham station. Golden Miller's former East Midland Saunders-Roe-bodied Leyland Tiger Cub ORR 345 was seen there on 8 April 1967. The board advertised 'Frequent Services to Staines Road, Bedfont'. (J. C. Gillham, Author's collection)

Golden Miller increased its bus fleet when Shepperton route 602 and Hanworth route 603 were introduced (from 1 February 1968) by acquiring two former Northern General 1957 Weymann-bodied Albion Aberdonians. CU 9758 was in the yard at Fern Grove, Feltham, ready to take up service on Bedfont route 601. (Michael Dryhurst)

Former Thames Valley Eastern Coach Works-bodied Bristol LL5G FMO 24 was photographed at the newly constructed terminus for route 601 on the west side of Bedfont Lane on 15 November 1968. (Tony Wright)

Seddon Motors had been a marginal participant in the bus manufacturing industry. A determined campaign to increase market share was launched in 1967 with its Pennine 4 model. Seddon's sales team must have considered that expanding Golden Miller was a good prospect and sent demonstrator RBU 502F, seen on the 601's stand at Feltham station on 28 November 1968, for trial. (Tony Wright)

Plaxton-bodied Bristol LH6L CJJ 44H had a good passenger loading as it departed from route 601's Feltham station bus stand in August 1971. (G. W. Morant, Author's collection)

8627 DT was one of two former Doncaster Corporation Roe-bodied AEC Reliances, which joined Golden Miller's fleet in November 1970. It was seen at the 601's Feltham station terminus on 21 December 1971. (Philip Wallis)

Above and below: A variety of vehicles could be found on Golden Miller's bus routes. Former SELNEC Park Royal-bodied Leyland Panther Cub BND 876C was working route 601 on Wednesday 7 February 1973 when it passed London Transport's MCW-bodied AEC Swift SMS 811 on the 116 at Bedfont Green. The next day former Western National Bristol LS5G MOD 952 was on the 601 when it overtook LT's SMS 789 at the same spot. (Both Tony Wright)

Above and below: Former City of Portsmouth Weymann-bodied Leyland Tiger Cub TTP 994 was about to turn right into route 601's Feltham station terminus on a wet 20 June 1973. Sister vehicle TTP 997 was seen turning off Staines Road into Hatton Road at Bedfont Green on 31 December 1973. Destination and route number displays for this 601 journey were noticeably absent. (Both Tony Wright)

Why Bristol RELH6G GEM 884N was parked on the south side of Feltham station displaying route 601 blind is unclear. Maybe the 601's normal stand north of the station was inaccessible or perhaps it was positioning to take up service on routes 602 or 603, which terminated south of the station. (Barry LeJeune)

Being a coach operator allowed Golden Miller to substitute coaches on its bus routes if pushed for vehicles. RPA 985E was a 1967 Duple-bodied Bedford VAM 14, which Golden Miller had acquired from Beach's of Staines in 1977. It was photographed on stand at Feltham station with a crude paper route number display in its windscreen. (Tony Wright)

Tellings-Golden Miller's Bristol RELL6G NLJ 827G was seen passing London Transport's Leyland National LS 351 at Bedfont Green on 14 March 1986. (Tony Wright)

Route 602 Feltham Station– Shepperton Station

The two ex-Northern General Albion Aberdonians were seen in the south yard at Feltham station. CU 9760 (left) was on route 602 to Shepperton whilst CU 9758 was working Hanworth route 603. (Laurie James collection)

Ex-Thames Valley Bristol LL5G FMO 24 was passing along Feltham High Street on 8 July 1970. (Tony Wright)

There was hiatus in route 602's operation between 13 May 1968 and 7 June 1969 when its service was reduced to operate between Feltham and Charlton Village (numbered 602A) with only two journeys going beyond to Shepperton. Strachan-bodied Ford R192 TUR 347E was displaying route number 602A at Feltham station. (Philip Wallis)

Above and below: Former Doncaster Corporation Roe-bodied AEC Reliance 8627 DT was seen at The Spelthorne, Ashford Common, working a southbound 602 journey on 1 September 1971. The other ex-Doncaster AEC Reliance 8629 DT displayed the almost all-blue livery applied by Golden Miller to most acquired buses. (Tony Wright, G. W. Morant, Author's collection)

Ex-Western National Eastern Coach Works-bodied Bristol LS5G MOD 952 was seen at the 602's terminus in the south yard at Feltham station on 21 December 1971. (Philip Wallis)

Former SELNEC Park Royal-bodied Leyland Panther Cub BND 868C was loading passengers in the south yard at Feltham station for a 602 journey to Shepperton. (Michael Dryhurst)

Plaxton-bodied Bedford YRQ SYO 602N was photographed at a Golden Miller bus stop in Shepperton during a 602 journey to Shepperton station. (Mark Worley)

Ex-Beach's of Staines Duple-bodied Bedford VAM14 coach RPA 985E was seen in the south yard at Feltham station loading passengers for a 602 journey. The coach was still in Beach's cream with red trim livery when photographed on 20 May 1977. (Tony Wright)

The rural nature along sections of route 602 is shown in this study of ex-Ribble Marshall-bodied Leyland Panther ARN 575C in front of Littleton Parish Church during a Feltham-bound journey. (Michael Dryhurst)

Above and below: Former City of Cardiff Alexander-bodied AEC Swift MBO 519F reached Golden Miller third-hand after a spell with Tappin of Wallingford. The bus was seen in Station Approach, Shepperton with what may have been an attempt at route identification on a small piece of paper in its windscreen. Alexander-bodied AEC Swift SRS 50K originated with Aberdeen Corporation in 1971 and was seen passing through Shepperton on a 602 journey with a functioning blind display. (Both Michael Dryhurst)

1968 Plaxton-bodied Bristol LH6L CJJ 44H was the veteran of Golden Miller's bus fleet when photographed in June 1982. Despite its age, this bus presented well when photographed outside the Shepperton premises of transport publisher Ian Allan Ltd. (Kevin Lane)

Although Caetano-bodied Volvo B10M C89 NNV is most readily associated with route 606 during the Tellings-Golden Miller era, it did see early use on route 602, as exemplified by this 1986 shot of that bus in Station Approach at Shepperton. (Laurie James)

London Buses' Leyland National LS 431 in the Westlink fleet, working a 117 journey to Ashford Hospital, passed former London Buses' Leyland National LS 328, then AYR 328T in Fountain Coaches fleet, on the 602 along Ashford Road at Lower Feltham. (Tony Wright)

After Fountain Coaches' collapse London Buses-controlled Westlink took up operation of the 602 from 9 April 1990. Minibus operation became routine, as shown by Carlyle-bodied Ford Transit FS 29 leaving Shepperton Studios on 24 April 1990 with Queen Mary Reservoir's embankment in the background. (Tony Wright)

Westlink ran the 602 until 28 August 1998, after which it was incorporated into extended route 400 operated by Arriva and Westlink. Eastern Coach Works-bodied Bristol LH6L BL 81 was photographed on stand at Feltham station. (Peter Bradley)

Route 603 Feltham Station–Hanworth

There was little space for boarding passengers in the south yard at Feltham station as Willowbrook-bodied
Bedford VAM70 KUJ 972F loaded for a 603 journey on 22 June 1970. A London Transport RF bus on route
237 stood behind with a Golden Miller Bristol LH coach in the background. (Philip Wallis)

Eastern Coach Works-bodied Bristol LS5G MOD 952 entered Golden Miller's service still painted in former owner Western National's green livery with fleet number 1681 intact. It was seen at Feltham station on 5 July 1971 with minimal route identification. (Tony Wright)

Former Bristol Omnibus Bristol LS5G XHW 405 was photographed at speed working a 603 journey along Castle Way, Hanworth, on 21 September 1972. (Tony Wright)

Golden Miller's Plaxton-bodied Bristol LH6L coach TMT 768F was substituting for a bus when working a 603 journey at the Oxford Arms in Bear Road, Hanworth, during December 1971. (Tony Wright)

Rear-engined Leyland Panther Cubs did not always prove popular with their original operators and so created good bargains on the second-hand market. Former SELNEC BND 876C (left) and BND 868C met at the entrance to Feltham station's south yard in July 1972. (Tony Wright)

This view shows the dual-door design of the Park Royal body on Panther Cub BND 876C as it proceeded along Feltham High Street bound for the station. (Philip Wallis)

Above and below: Route 603's loop terminal routing at Hanworth changed several times in the 1970s due to road construction works. The 'Brown Bear' pub, at the junction of Bear Road and the A 316 Sunbury Way, was the designated terminus between 1970 and 1973. Former Doncaster Corporation AEC Reliance 8627 DT was seen passing that establishment on 30 August 1972. The 'Brown Bear' was demolished in 1973 to allow construction of a slipway to the A 316. Former SELNEC Park Royal-bodied Leyland Tiger Cub 3651 NE was emerging from Bear Road past the former pub's site. (Both Tony Wright)

Plaxton-bodied Bedford YRQ trio SYO 600-2N formed the backbone of Golden Miller's bus fleet from the mid-1970s. SYD 601N was descending Feltham High Street bound for Hanworth in 1975. (Philip Wallis)

ARN 575C was a former Ribble Marshall-bodied Leyland Leopard photographed in July 1981 along Sunbury Way, Hanworth, heading to Feltham. (Tony Wright)

Former Cardiff Corporation Alexander-bodied AEC Swift MBO 519F was particularly disadvantaged for showing route information with a painted-over destination box! A number of passengers on board had recognised this was the 603 bus as it emerged from Elmwood Avenue's junction with Feltham High Street on 3 March 1983. (Tony Wright)

Plaxton-bodied Bedford YRQ SYO 602N displayed Golden Miller's two-tone blue and cream livery applied to some buses as it rested at Feltham station between 603 journeys in May 1982. (Kevin Lane)

Route 603 passed through Feltham Garrison. Former Grampian Alexander-bodied AEC Swift SRS 50K was seen on 4 March 1983 at the point where the Garrison Railway crossed Elmwood Avenue. (Tony Wright)

Telling-Golden Miller's former Devon General Eastern Coach Works-bodied Bristol RELL6G POD 826H was at Feltham station before starting a 603 journey. (Laurie James)

Fountain Coaches operated route 603 from 22 October 1985 until its last day of operation on 7 June 1986. Plaxton-bodied Leyland Leopard HUP 131N was seen in the south yard at Feltham station. (Tony Wright)

Route 604 Walton-on-Thames–Station
(Oatlands Village from 7 December 1970)

The Walton-on-Thames Motor Company's (WOTMC) service between town and railway station ran daily until April 1962. 1937 Willmott-bodied Bedford WTB DLD 407 was seen in the town on a Sunday in 1952. (C. Carter, Author's Collection)

JDF 306 was a 1949 Mulliner-bodied Bedford OB photographed outside WOTMC's premises at the junction of Bridge Street and New Zealand Avenue in the town. (Michael Dryhurst)

WOTMC's route ran in parallel with London Transport route 218 and used LT bus stops, apart from the spur along Station Avenue. 1948 Duple-bodied Bedford OB MPG 750 had pulled up at a LT request stop. (Michael Dryhurst)

Duple-bodied Bedford OB OPJ 200 was new to WOTMC in 1950 and was the last bus in service with successor Walton Lodge Garage until a prohibition notice was issued by a Ministry of Transport vehicle inspector in October 1970. It was photographed earlier at Walton-on-Thames station. (Philip Wallis)

Golden Miller's Eastern Coach Works-bodied Bristol LS5G XHW 405 was seen in Hepworth Way, Walton-on-Thames, in July 1971. (Michael Dryhurst)

Bristol LS5G MOD 952 had been repainted into Golden Miller's blue with cream relief livery when this picture was taken in Walton-on-Thames with destination blind set for a 604 journey beyond the station to Oatlands Village. (Michael Dryhurst)

Route 604 was reduced to Monday to Friday peak hours operation from 7 May 1973. The 604 bus returned to Feltham between peaks to layover on the 601's stand north of the station. The pair of ex-Portsmouth Leyland Tiger Cubs TTP 994/7 were photographed at lunchtime on 5 November 1974, whilst former SELNEC Leyland Tiger Cub 3651 NE operated the 604 route, and Bristol LH6L CJJ 44H the 601 on 25 November 1974. (Both Tony Wright)

Walton-on-Thames station remained unserved by buses for around nine months following Mole Valley's discontinuance of its service in June 1975. A link to the station was restored when London Transport diverted Monday to Friday journeys on route 218 (Kingston–Staines) off Hersham Road to double-run to the station from 10 April 1976. LT's RF 369 was seen at the station stand once occupied by WOTMC's Bedfords. (Michael Dryhurst)

Route 606 Staines–Stanwell Moor (including Stanwell Schools route 605)

London Transport's route 203 was the established link between Staines and Stanwell. RF 420 was photographed in Bridge Street, Staines, working a Sunday shuttle service to and from Stanwell on 24 July 1966. Re-routing of the 203 away from Stanwell Village from 11 March 1972 gave Golden Miller's 606 exclusivity in that area. (Philip Wallis)

Golden Miller's Eastern Coach Works-bodied Bristol LS5G MOD 962 was photographed on stand at Staines station on 21 December 1971 with a London Country RT behind. Ex-Doncaster AEC Reliance 8627 DT was seen at the same terminus on another day. (Philip Wallis, Tony Wright)

MOD 962 had suffered a drastic deterioration in route information display as it passed through Stanwell Moor on a 606 journey on 28 September 1972. (Tony Wright)

Above and below: After the 606 was extended across Staines from 15 May 1972, Golden Miller joined London Transport and London Country in using the forecourt of former Staines West station in Moor Lane for turning buses and layover. Bristol LS5G MOD 952 stood alongside LT's SMS 640 and RF 449. Another bus line up there comprised Golden Miller's Bristol LH6L CJJ 44H with LT's RFs 324 and 525 behind and a route 117 Routemaster in the background. (Both Tony Wright)

Plaxton-bodied Bedford YRQ SYO 600N was seen passing The Wheatsheaf pub in Park Road, Stanwell, shortly after delivery to Golden Miller in September 1974. (Tony Wright)

Former SELNEC Leyland Tiger Cub 3651 NE had good passenger loading, despite not displaying any route identification, as it passed along Clare Road, Stanwell, on 2 October 1974. (Tony Wright)

Former Greater Glasgow Alexander-bodied Leyland Atlantean SGD 586 had myriad route number displays when photographed turning out of Hithermoor Road at Stanwell Moor on 3 December 1976 but was probably deployed on Stanwell School's route 605. (Tony Wright)

Leyland Nationals had superseded AEC Swifts on LT's route 116 when this picture was taken of LT's LS 42 and RFs 381/512 alongside Golden Miller's Bedford YRQ SYO 600N on the forecourt of former Staines West station. The 218 and 219 were LT's last RF-operated bus routes until that type's withdrawal after 30 March 1979. (Michael Dryhurst)

Above and below: Plaxton-bodied Bristol RELH6G GEM 884N was seen heading out of Staines along London Road during summer 1978. This bus had a most unusual background, being new in 1969 to P. Doyle Ltd of Roundwood, Co Wicklow, Republic of Ireland, where it was registered ONI 300. Doyle traded as St Kevin's Bus Service with a principal bus route between Dublin and Glendalough along which ONI 300 was photographed climbing from Kilmacanogue to Calary in the Wicklow Hills. (Both Michael Dryhurst)

Staines High Street on a dismal winter's day saw Golden Miller's Duple-bodied Bedford YMT ELA 389T on the 606 being passed by London Country's Leyland National SNB 245. (Michael Dryhurst)

Marshall-bodied Leyland Leopard ARN 575C was photographed passing through Stanwell on 11 March 1980. (Tony Wright)

Alexander-bodied AEC Swift MBO 519F displayed a reasonably large 'Staines & Stanwell Moor 606' notice in its windscreen when on stand at Staines bus station on 20 May 1982. (Tony Wright)

Quite why Bedford YRQ SYO 602N had a route 603 blind display at the old Staines West station is not known. Perhaps it had arrived to replace Bristol LH6L CJJ 44H as the 606 route bus when the pair were photographed on 30 June 1982. (Tony Wright)

Tellings-Golden Miller's Eastern Coach Works-bodied Bristol RELL6G FVX 614H was on stand at Staines bus station during 1985. (Laurie James)

Volvo B10M C89 NNV was the regular 606 bus for a number of years. This former Caetano demonstrator was seen in Stanwell shortly after acquisition by Tellings-Golden Miller in 1986. (John F. Simons, Stephen Telling Collection)

Photographs of C188 RVV in service with Tellings-Golden Miller are scarce since it was only in the fleet for just over one year. This Caetano-bodied Volvo B10M was approaching Staines bus station on 10 June 1987, shortly before sale to Hutchison's Coaches of Overtown, Lanarkshire. (Alec Swain, Kevin Lane Collection)

Tellings-Golden Miller had allocated Jonckheere-bodied Volvo B10M-61 D319 VVV to work the 606 when that coach was photographed alongside London Busline's Plaxton Beaver-bodied Mercedes-Benz 811D 631 at Staines bus station. (Tony Wright)

C89 NNV was repainted into the white, yellow and blue livery that would become the hallmark of Tellings-Golden Miller's expanded operations. It was seen on stand at Staines bus station. (Laurie James)

London & Country's East Lancs-bodied Dennis Dart DS 19 was seen loading in Staines bus station for a 606 journey on 20 June 1996. (Philip Wallis)

Route 600 Bedfont–Feltham–Hanworth

Isleworth Coaches' first venture into bus operation saw its ex-London Transport RTL 633 (KGU 83) near Richmond station working Richmond Hill route 235 on 24 February 1966 during LT's industrial dispute. LT's RT 1111 behind was working a route 90B journey to Kew Gardens station. (Michael Dryhurst)

Isleworth Coaches' ex-London Transport RT 4790 (OLD 827) indicated that operator's further bus route aspirations with its Isleworth & District fleet name. It was passing Acton Town station on contract or private work when photographed on 16 July 1969. (J. C. Gillham, Author's Collection)

Fountain Coaches' first dedicated bus for route 600 was former Trimdon Motor Services Willowbrook-bodied Leyland Leopard HUP 131N seen in Feltham on 15 August 1986 with no route number display. (Gerald Mead)

Fountain Coaches' former South Midland Bristol RELH6L RBW 83M displayed route number 600 as it passed along Feltham High Street. (Laurie James)

Former Bexleybus Leyland National YYE 282T had Fountain Bus fleet name on its side panel but no route identification as it passed along Nailhead Road on the 600's inbound route to Hanworth. (Tony Wright)

Westlink's Leyland National LS 145 was negotiating Feltham station's level crossing in Bedfont Lane, which often disrupted the 600's schedule. (Tony Wright)

Westlink's Leyland National LS 270 was photographed at the bus stand north of Feltham station where a LT bus stop had been erected. (Peter Bradley)

London United's wheelchair-accessible Reeve Burgess-bodied Iveco 49.10 FS 8 displayed evidence of route H25's Hounslow Council funding on its side panel when seen at Butts Farm, Hanworth. (Philip Wallis)

Route H25 has just been converted to low-floor bus operation when Wright Crusader-bodied Dennis Dart SLF CD 4 was photographed at Hatton Cross on 16 November 1996. (Philip Wallis)

Route 116 Brentford–Bedfont Green

The 116 was an old established London bus route that once ran to Windsor. Westlink was its operator prior to TGM Buses taking up the LRT contract on 10 August 1991. Leyland National LS 206 was seen in London Road, Hounslow, on 11 June 1991. (Mike Harris)

3561 was photographed along London Road, Hounslow, on 10 August 1991, TGM Buses' first day of operation of route 116. This Leyland National originated in Lancashire United's fleet. (Mike Harris)

Leyland National 3598 came to TGM Buses from Midland Red (North) but originated in the main Midland Red fleet before that concern was divided into parts for National Bus Company privatisation. It was passing Isleworth station in August 1991. (Kevin Lane)

Leyland must have considered that expanding Tellings-Golden Miller was a good sales prospect when it sent Leyland Lynx demonstrator H48 NDU, seen in Hounslow on 25 August 1991, for evaluation. (Mike Harris)

During its vehicle crisis TGM Buses was helped out with the loan of buses from other Drawlane Group fleets. 3829, seen leaving Hounslow bus station on 8 September 1991, was a Midland Fox Leyland National. (Mike Harris)

Leyland National 3634 retained blue and white colours but had lost its TGM Buses fleet name and legal lettering when seen in London & Country ownership along Hounslow High Street on 12 September 1992. (Mike Harris)

National Greenways were mid-life Leyland Nationals fitted with new East Lancashire Coachbuilders bodywork. London & Country's 748, seen passing Hounslow bus station, originated as a 1974 Leyland National with West Yorkshire, registered GUA 821N. It was rebuilt in 1993 as a Greenway and re-registered NIW 6508. (Philip Wallis)

Route 117 Brentford–Staines

The 117 was another long-established London bus route. As with the 116, Westlink operated it prior to TGM Buses taking over from 10 August 1991. Leyland National LS 251 was photographed in Hounslow High Street a month earlier. (Mike Harris)

TGM Buses Leyland National 3562 displayed a distinctive horseshoe motif, linking Telling-Golden Miller's name with the celebrated 1930s racehorse Golden Miller, as it loaded passengers in Feltham High Street on 10 August 1991. (Mike Harris)

3663 was one of several Leyland Nationals that had originated in Midland Red's fleet. It was seen at Brentford County Court on 10 August 1991. (Mike Harris)

Leyland National 3551 still displayed TGM Buses fleet name and motif when seen in Staines Street on 16 May 1992 after passing into London & Country ownership. (Mike Harris)

SNB 475 was a typical Leyland National from London & Country's main fleet. This 1979 bus was seen at Staines bus station working a 117 journey on 16 May 1992. (Mike Harris)

TGM Buses 3598 is illustrated previously on route 116. The same bus was photographed along Hounslow High Street on 18 April 1993 after repainting into London & Country colours as fleet number 598. (Mike Harris)

London & Country's National Greenway 347 started life as Leyland National 3620 with Hants & Dorset in 1974. It re-emerged as a Greenway in February 1993 and was photographed two months later in Staines bus station. (Mike Harris)

Contract Work and Garages

Former Potteries Motor Traction NEH 446 had an export-model Leyland Titan OPD2/1 chassis, which was lengthened and re-bodied with a Northern Counties double-deck body in 1955. It was much used on school contracts and was photographed along Bedfont Lane, Feltham, on 28 February 1966. (Tony Wright)

BDJ 801 was a 1952 Park Royal-bodied AEC Regent 111 identical to contemporary London Transport RT types. It was seen leaving Wembley Stadium carrying a party of schoolboys away from an event at that popular venue. (Author's Collection)

A glimpse inside Golden Miller's Fern Grove yard at Feltham on 9 May 1973 revealed ex-Manchester City Transport and SELNEC Leyland Panther Cub BND 868C and former Western National Bristol LS5G MOD 952. (Tony Wright)

Sometimes Golden Miller vehicles parked in Nursery Close, next to Fern Grove, where ex-Greater Glasgow Leyland Atlantean SGD 586 was seen. (Tony Wright)

Ex-City of Portsmouth Leyland Tiger Cub TTP 997 was seen in Stanwell on a school contract journey on 17 January 1975. This working was possibly the precursor for Stanwell Schools route 605 introduced on 6 September 1976. (Tony Wright)

Golden Miller was a regular participant at Bus Rallies. New Duple-bodied Bedford YMT ELA 389T made a fine display at Showbus 1979 in Hillingdon. (Mark Worley)

Tellings-Golden Miller's yard at Wintersells Road at Byfleet in 1986 revealed ex-Devon General Bristol RELL6G TUO 255J, former National Travel Jonckheere-bodied Volvo B10M-61 coach ONV 649Y, Caetano-bodied Volvo B10M-61 bus C89 NNV and an unidentified coach. (Laurie James)

Although displaying route number 603, TGM's former Eastern National Bristol RELL6G FVX 614H was on hire to British Railways for rail replacement duty when photographed at West Byfleet station. (Mark Worley)

Golden Miller Coaches

Fred Varney's Golden Miller is recalled by 1931 Duple-bodied Gilford AS6 PL 5879. It was new to Ham Bros of Richmond and passed to Golden Miller in 1947, remaining in its fleet until 1951. (The Omnibus Society)

Above and below: F. G. Wilder's Golden Miller favoured Bristol chassis for its coaches, taking twenty new Plaxton- or Duple-bodied LHs between 1968 and 1976. Plaxton-bodied Bristol LH6Ps YGK 764G and DGU 865H were seen parked on route 601's stand at Feltham station and in the south yard respectively in June 1970. (Both Philip Wallis)

57-seat Caetano-bodied Seddon Pennine 6 LMP 977K joined Golden Miller's fleet in 1972. (The Omnibus Society)

1969 Duple-bodied Bedford VAM 70 ROT 351G was acquired by Golden Miller from Beach's of Staines. It retained Beach's red and cream livery when photographed along Staines Road West. (Tony Wright)

Telling's Coaches and Tellings-Golden Miller Coaches

Stephen Telling was seen with his first coach: 1966 Duple-bodied Bedford VAM14 MYN 597D ex-Ben Stanley Coaches. Tellings Coaches' first job in 1972 was a school party trip from Weybridge to Winchester. (Stephen Telling Collection)

Plaxton Viewmaster-bodied Volvo B58 TGD 991R was cautiously disembarking from Red Funnel's cross-Solent ferry at Cowes, Isle of Wight. Wooden blocks were used to prevent the front of the coach grounding on the slipway. (Stephen Telling Collection)

Above and below: Tellings Coaches specialised in European tours. Plaxton Supreme-bodied Volvo B58 NLC 873V was photographed in the early 1980s at St Wolfgang, Austria, whilst 1984 Jonckheere-bodied Volvo B10M B520 CBD was seen elsewhere. (Both Stephen Telling)

Volvo coaches figured prominently in Tellings-Golden Miller's fleet. E502 KNV was a 51-seat Jonckheere-bodied Volvo B10M-61 seen at the port of Dover in June 1992 after disembarking from a trip to Eurodisney, Paris. (Kevin Lane)

Tellings-Golden Miller's immaculate Jonckheere-bodied Volvo B10M-62 L10 TGM was photographed along the A30 London Road near Ashford Hospital on 2 April 1994, shortly after delivery. (Philip Wallis)

Van Hool-bodied Volvo B10M T9 TGM proudly proclaimed that Tellings-Golden Miller had been voted Coach Operator of the Year 1999 (Class 17-40 vehicles) by *Route One* magazine. Note the motif linking the company with champion racehorse Golden Miller. (Stephen Telling Collection)

21-seat Caetano-bodied Toyota N60 TGM was one of the smaller coaches in TGM's fleet when photographed leaving Staines bus station on 27 August 2001. (Philip Wallis)

Cardiff Bluebird Bus Routes 1993–1996

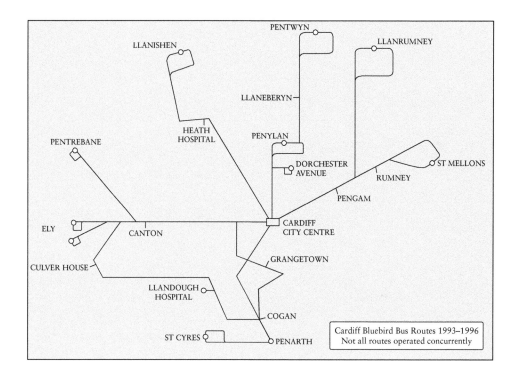

PENTWYN

LLANRUMNEY

LLANISHEN

LLANEBERYN

HEATH
HOSPITAL

PENYLAN

PENTREBANE

DORCHESTER
AVENUE

ST MELLONS

RUMNEY

PENGAM

ELY

CANTON

CARDIFF
CITY CENTRE

CULVER HOUSE

GRANGETOWN

LLANDOUGH
HOSPITAL

COGAN

ST CYRES

PENARTH

Cardiff Bluebird Bus Routes 1993–1996
Not all routes operated concurrently

Cardiff Bluebird

Former Greater Manchester Northern Counties-bodied Leyland Atlantean 62 was seen passing along Grand Avenue, Ely, on 26 March 1994 working Cardiff Bluebird's first route 218. (Philip Wallis)

Roe-bodied Leyland Atlantean 64, photographed in Grand Avenue, Ely, on 26 March 1994, came from South Yorkshire's fleet. (Philip Wallis)

Above and below: Seven former London Buses MCW Metroriders joined Cardiff Bluebird. 32 was turning into Wood Street and 34 turning from Westgate Street into Park Street on 26 March 1994. (Both Philip Wallis)

Three former East Midlands MCW Metroriders served with Cardiff Bluebird. 33 was seen in Wood Street before renumbering to 42. (Stephen Telling Collection)

16-seat Dormobile-bodied Ford Transit 40 was deployed on the St Mellons route alongside 75/78-seat double-deckers. (Philip Wallis)

Above and below: Four former London Buses' DMS-type Leyland Fleetlines saw service with Cardiff Bluebird. 59 carried previous operator G. K. Kinch's livery whilst 60 entered service all-over white. (Both Philip Wallis)

Four former City of Nottingham Leyland Fleetlines ran for Cardiff Bluebird. The distinctive style of their Nottingham-influenced East Lancs-bodywork was evident as 19 departed from Wood Street terminus on 22 October 1994 and 8 (formerly 18) negotiated city centre streets on 20 January 1996. (Both Philip Wallis)

Route 302 to Penarth and St Cyres was a short-lived service withdrawn after 30 December 1994. Dormobile-bodied Ford Transit minibus 44 was seen at Wood Street terminus on 22 October 1994. (Philip Wallis)

Above and below: Two former Alexander-bodied MCW Metrobuses came from Black Prince of Morley, having originated with West Yorkshire PTE. 70 was negotiating the city centre terminal loop and 71 was on stand at Wood Street on 11 February 1995. (Both Philip Wallis)

A grouping of Cardiff Bluebird buses at Wood Street on 11 February 1995 was headed by MCW Metroriders 80 and 38, originally with South Wales and London Buses respectively. (Philip Wallis)

The Plaxton Pointer-bodied Dennis Dart was the best-selling single-deck combination of its time. Cardiff Bluebird's 1 was seen along Wood Street on 9 September 1995. (Philip Wallis)

Above and below: MCW Metrobus 53 displayed Cardiff Bluebird's new blue livery whilst Leyland Atlantean 63 retained original white and blue colours when both buses passed along Westgate Street on 9 September 1995. (Both Philip Wallis)

Batches of Reeve Burgess-bodied Dodge S56s comprised the last midibuses to join Cardiff Bluebird. 92, in Wood Street, had originated with Manchester Minibuses. (Stephen Telling Collection)

Latterly some Cardiff Bluebird buses were equipped with day-glo yellow destination blinds. MCW Metrobus 52 displayed more comprehensive route details, as shown on these blinds. (Stephen Telling Collection)

A broadside view of former Trent Eastern Coach Works-bodied Leyland Atlantean 67 (ONN 574P) taken in Cardiff Bluebird's Penarth Road yard at Grangetown. (Stephen Telling Collection)

Cardiff Bluebird participated in the Traws Cambria service (jointly with Crosville) under the Coach Travel Centre identity. Duple-bodied Leyland Tiger 71 was photographed along Wood Street on 9 July 1994 at the start of its long journey to Birkenhead. (Philip Wallis)

Tellings-Golden Miller Expansion

MCW Metrorider E804 UDT and new Plaxton Beaver-bodied Mercedes-Benz 709D M70 TGM were seen at Sutton station on 8 April 1995 on the first day of operation of LRT-contracted route S3. (Philip Wallis)

The 513 was a circuitous Surrey CC-sponsored route linking communities once served by London Transport's Central and Country Buses. Plaxton Beaver-bodied Mercedes-Benz 709D P70 TGM was photographed in Kingston. (Philip Wallis)

A trio of TGM buses working Surrey CC-contracted routes met in Esher High Street on 15 July 1997. MCW Metrorider E808 UDT headed Mercedes-Benz P70 TGM and MCW Metrorider E224 PWY. The two Metroriders had seen earlier service with Cardiff Bluebird. (Philip Wallis)

Award of the LRT contract for route 235 gave Tellings-Golden Miller its first mainstream London bus route. R502 SJM, seen at Hounslow in March 1998, was one of twelve Plaxton Pointer-bodied Dennis Dart SLFs allocated to the 235's weekday operation. (Kevin Lane)

Award of TfL's route 203 contract brought Tellings-Golden Miller back into traditional territory once covered by Golden Miller route 606. Plaxton Pointer 2-bodied Dennis Dart SLF W402 UGM was seen along Clare Road, Stanwell, on 1 September 2001, inaugural day of TGM's operation. (Philip Wallis)

The UK's contemporary road vehicle registration system came into effect from 1 September 2001. TGM's Dennis Dart SLF 417 (RX51 FGM) was amongst the first buses to display 'year dating' on its number plate when photographed at Ashford Hospital that same day. (Philip Wallis)

F. G. Wilder & Sons Ltd (t/a Golden Miller Services) and Tellings-Golden Miller Ltd Buses Used on Routes 601–606 and Earlier Double-Deck Buses

Reg. No	Chassis	Bodywork	Former Owner	Year	Date In	Date Out
FOF 211	Daimler COG5	MCCW H54R	Lovegroves, Silchester	1939	7/1959	7/1960
BDJ 801	AEC Regent 111 (RT-type)	Park Royal H56R	St Helens Corporation D1	1952	1/1962	2/1964
NEH 446	Leyland OPD2/1	Northern Counties L55RD	Potteries L 446	1949	12/1963	7/1966
ORR 345	Leyland PSUC1/1	Saunders-Roe B44F	East Midland R345	1954	6/1966	By 4/1969
CU 9760	Albion MR11N	Weymann B44F	Northern General 1760	1957	2/1968	By 2/1970
CU 9758	Albion MR11N	Weymann B44F	Northern General 1758	1957	4/1968	By 12/1969
FMO 24	Bristol LL5G	Eastern Coach Works FB39F	Thames Valley 820	See notes	4/1968	12/1971
TUR 347E	Ford R192	Strachan B46F	Knight, Hemel Hempstead	1967	11/1968	8/1971
RBU 502F	Seddon Pennine 4	Seddon B45F	Manufacturer's Demonstrator	1968	On trial 11/1968	
KUJ 972F	Bedford VAM70	Willowbrook B45F	Hampson, Oswestry	1967	5/1969	4/1971
CJJ 44H	Bristol LH6L	Plaxton B49F	See notes	1968	11/1969	By 9/1985
8627 DT	AEC Reliance	Roe B45F	Doncaster Corporation 27	1961	11/1970	11/1972
8629 DT	AEC Reliance	Roe B45F	Doncaster Corporation 29	1961	11/1970	12/1971

Reg. No	Chassis	Bodywork	Former Owner	Year	Date In	Date Out
XHW 405	Bristol LS5G	Eastern Coach Works B45F	Bristol Omnibus 2889	1956	12/1970	12/1972
MOD 952	Bristol LS5G	Eastern Coach Works B41F	Tillingbourne Valley	1952	7/1971	7/1974
MOD 962	Bristol LS5G	Eastern Coach Works B41F	Western National 1671	1953	9/1971	12/1972
BND 876C	Leyland Panther Cub	Park Royal B43D	SELNEC 31	1965	12/1971	12/1974
BND 868C	Leyland Panther Cub	Park Royal B43D	SELNEC 23	1965	2/1972	11/1974
TTP 994	Leyland PSUC1/1	Weymann B34D	City of Portsmouth 20	1960	11/1972	1/1976
3651 NE	Leyland PSUC1/12	Park Royal DP40F	SELNEC 6	1962	12/1972	7/1975
TTP 997	Leyland PSUC1/1	Weymann B34D	City of Portsmouth 23	1960	7/1973	1/1976
SYO 600N	Bedford YRQ	Plaxton B37F	New	1974	9/1974	By 4/1985
SYO 601N	Bedford YRQ	Plaxton B37F	New	1974	9/1974	By 4/1985
SYO 602N	Bedford YRQ	Plaxton B37F	New	1974	9/1974	By 4/1985
GEM 884N	Bristol RELH6G	Plaxton B55F	Davies, Halewood	1969	9/1975	12/1978
SGD 586	Leyland PDR1/1	Alexander H44/34F	Greater Glasgow PTE LA 6	1962	8/1976	11/1978
ARN 575C	Leyland PSU3/1R	Marshall B53F	Ribble 575	1965	10/1978	2/1982
ELA 389T	Bedford YMT	Duple B63F	New	1979	1/1979	By 9/1985
MBO 519F	AEC Swift	Alexander B47D	Tappin, Wallingford	1968	4/1982	By 6/1985
SRS 50K	AEC Swift	Alexander B43D	Grampian Regional Transport 50	1971	9/1982	By 6/1985
FVX 614H	Bristol RELL6G	Eastern Coach Works B53F	Eastern National 1512	1969	4/1985	By 3/1986

Reg. No	Chassis	Bodywork	Former Owner	Year	Date In	Date Out
LNN 93K	Bristol RELH6G	Eastern Coach Works C47F	East Midland 93	1972	5/1985	By 5/1986
NLJ 827G	Bristol RELL6G	Eastern Coach Works DP50F	T and K Coaches, Ilford	1969	6/1985	3/1986
TUO 255J	Bristol RELL6G	Eastern Coach Works B53F	Kinch, Barrow	1970	By 4/1985	By 5/1986
POD 826H	Bristol RELL6G	Eastern Coach Works B53F	Devon General 2727	1969	6/1985	By 5/1986
C89 NNV	Volvo B10M-61	Caetano B57F	Ex Caetano Demonstrator	1985	1/1986	3/1995
C188 RVV	Volvo B10M-61	Caetano B52F	New	1986	5/1986	7/1987
J45 GGB	Leyland Lynx 11	Leyland B51F	Whitelaw, Stonehouse	1992	Late 1993	Early 1994

Original Operators:

FOF 211: Birmingham Corporation 1211. NEH 446: Original body Weymann B35F. Chassis lengthened in 1955 to 30 feet and re-seated B39F. Later in 1955 re-bodied with 1951 Northern Counties L55RD from Potteries Leyland TD4 L 59.

FMO 24: Bristol L6B/Windover C33F new 3/1950 as Thames Valley 549. Chassis re-built by Thames Valley to LL5G configuration and re-bodied Eastern Coach Works FB39F. Re-entered Thames Valley service 2/1959 re-numbered 820.

CJJ 44H: Chassis originally used by Bristol Commercial Vehicles for development work.

XHW 405: Bristol Tramways 2889. MOD 952: Western National 1661.

BND 868C and BND 876C: Manchester City Transport 68 and 76 respectively.

3651 NE: Manchester Corporation 51. GEM 884N: Doyle, Roundwood, Republic of Ireland, 8/1969 registered ONI 300. Sold to Davies, Halewood, 4/1975 and re-registered GEM 884N.

MBO 519F: City of Cardiff 519. SRS 50K: Aberdeen Corporation Transport 50.

NLJ 827G: Hants & Dorset 1612 then Hampshire Bus 1612 from 4/1983

TUO 255J: Western National 2743. POD 826H: Western National 2727.

J45 GGB was on loan whilst C89 NNV was being repainted.

Fountain Coaches Ltd
Vehicles Recorded as Used on Bus Routes 600, 601 and 603

Reg No	Chassis	Bodywork	Former Owner	Year	Date In	Date Out
PGW 656L	Leyland Leopard	Plaxton C47F	Isleworth Coches	1973	3/1986	5/1990
HUP 131N	Leyland Leopard	Plaxton B55F	Borehamwood Travel	1975	3/1986	By 5/1989
RBW 83M	Bristol RELH6L	Eastern Coach Works DP49F	South Midland 83	1974	6/1986	By 5/1990
AYR 328T	Leyland National	Leyland National B36D	Bexleybus 62	1978	1/1989	5/1990
YYE 282T	Leyland National	Leyland National B36D	Bexleybus 57	1978	2/1989	5/1990
KJD 527P	Leyland National	Leyland National B36D	London Buses LS 27	1976	4/1989	5/1990

Original Operators:
PGW 656L: Grey Green Coaches. HUP 131N: Trimdon Motor Services. RBW 83M: City of Oxford 83. AYR 328T: London Transport Executive LS 328. YYE 282T: London Transport Executive LS 282. KJD 527P: London Transport Executive LS 27 (on dealer hire).

Bexleybus was a division of London Buses Ltd, a subsidiary of London Regional Transport.

TGM Buses
Vehicles Used on London Regional
Transport-contracted Routes 116 and 117

Fleet No	Reg No	Chassis/Bodywork	Former Owner	Year	Date In	Date Out
3562	NOE 562R	Leyland National B49F	Midland Fox	1976	7/1991	1/1992
3634	SGR 134R	Leyland National B49F	Midland Fox	1977	3/1991	1/1992
3598	NOE 598R	Leyland National B49F	Midland Red (North)	1977	5/1991	1/1992
3561	NEN 961R	Leyland National B49F	Private Owner	1977	5/1991	1/1992
3038	VPT 950R	Leyland National B49F	North (dealer)	1977	9/1991	1/1992
3638	PUK 638R	Leyland National B49F	Loughborough Coach & Bus	1977	4/1991	1/1992
3641	PUK 641R	Leyland National B49F	Loughborough Coach & Bus	1977	7/1991	1/1992
3643	PUK 643R	Leyland National B49F	Loughborough Coach & Bus	1977	6/1991	1/1992
3654	PUK 654R	Leyland National B49F	Loughborough Coach & Bus	1977	7/1991	1/1992
3663	SOA 663S	Leyland National B49F	Loughborough Coach & Bus	1978	7/1991	1/1992
3760	XNG 760S	Leyland National B49F	Cambus	1978	6/1991	1/1992
3713	TOF 713S	Leyland National B49F	Loughborough Coach & Bus	1978	6/1991	1/1992
3715	TOF 715S	Leyland National B49F	Loughborough Coach & Bus	1978	4/1991	1/1992
3551	ERP 551T	Leyland National B49F	Midland Fox	1979	5/1991	1/1992
	H48 NDU	Leyland Lynx B51F	Manufacturer's demonstrator	1990	On trial 8/1991	

3799	LUP 899T	Leyland National B49F	North (dealer)	1979	9/1991	1/1992
3821	BVP 821V	Leyland National B49F	Loughborough Coach & Bus (on hire)	1980	9/1991	10/1991
3829	EON 829V	Leyland National B49F	Loughborough Coach & Bus (on hire)	1980	9/1991	10/1991

TGM fleet numbers were in the Midland Fox series. Loughborough Coach & Bus was a subsidiary of Midland Fox.

Original Operators:
3562, 3598, 3638, 3641, 3643, 3654, 3663, 3713, 3715, 3821, 3829: Midland Red 562, 598, 638, 641, 643, 654, 663, 713, 715, 821, 829 respectively. 3038, 3634, 3799: United Automobile 3038, 3034, 3099 respectively. 3551: United Counties 551. 3561: Lancashire United 474. 3760: Eastern Counties LN 760.

3562, 3634, 3598, 3561, 3038, 3641, 3654, 3663, 3760, 3713, 3715, 3551, 3799 passed to London Country Bus (South West) Ltd (t/a London & Country) in 1/1992.

Tellings-Golden Miller Ltd Trading as Cardiff Bluebird and Cardiff Bluebird Ltd Bus Fleet List

Fleet Nos	Reg Nos	Chassis/Bodywork	Year	Original Operator
1 /2	M100/200 CBB	Dennis Dart 9.8 SDL/ Plaxton B40F	1995	New
8 – 11 (originally 18 -21)	MAU 618 -21P	Leyland Atlantean/East Lancs H47/31D	1975	City of Nottingham 618/9/20/1
17	E837 BTN	MCW Metrorider DP25F	1988	Northumbria 836
18/19	D708/9 TWM	Dodge S56/Northern Counties B22F	1987	Merseyside 7708/9
21/2/4/5	D861/2/4/5 NVS	Dodge S56/Reeve Burgess B25F	1986	London Country (North West) MDB 20/1/3/4
26	F116 EKO	MCW Metrorider B25F	1988	Maidstone 252
31/2/4/8/9 47/9	E631/2/4/138/ 639 KYW/ D477/69 PON	MCW Metrorider B25F (47/9 B23F)	1987	London Buses MR 31/2/34/8/39/9/17
33	F101 YYB	MCW Metrorider B25F	1988	London Buses MR 101
40	C35 WBF	Ford Transit/Dormobile B16F	1986	Midland Red (North) 35
41 - 5	C437/8/41/4/7 BHY	Ford Transit/Dormobile B16F	1986	Bristol 7437/8/41/4/7
41/2/8 (42 originally 33)	E811/2/08 UDT	MCW Metrorider B25F	1987	East Midland 811/2/08
44	E604 VKC	MCW Metrorider B25F	1987	Smith, Prenton
46	E232 PWY	MCW Metrorider B23F	1987	Yorkshire Rider 2032
51 – 4/59	JHE 141/3/63/ 4/39W	MCW Metrobus/MCW H46/31F	1981	South Yorkshire 1843/63/4/39/41

57 – 60	OJD 434/44/55R/ THX 305S	Leyland Fleetline/Park Royal H44/24D	1977	London Transport DMS 2434/44/55/ 2305
61/3/4	DWY 563V/ XWG 652T/CWG 760V	Leyland Atlantean/Roe H45/29D	1979	South Yorkshire 1737/1652/1760
62/5/6	LJA 641P/ KBU 911/5P	Leyland Atlantean/ Northern Counties H43/32F	1975	Greater Manchester 7641/7580/4
67	ONN 574P	Leyland Atlantean/ Eastern Coach Works H43/31F	1976	Trent 574
71/8 (78 originally 70)	UWW 519/18X	MCW Metrobus/ Alexander H45/33F	1982	West Yorkshire PTE 7519/8)
72	ULS 621X	MCW Metrobus/ Alexander H45/33F	1982	Alexander (Midland) MRM 21
80 - 3	E261/2/9/70 REP	MCW Metrorider B23F	1987	South Wales 261/2/9/70
90/2	D420/12 NNA	Dodge S56/Reeve Burgess B22F	1987	Manchester Minibuses 3420/12
93	D563 RCK	Mercedes-Benz 608D/ Reeve Burgess B20F	1986	Ribble 563
130	MHS 30P	Leyland Leopard/ Alexander B53F	1976	Central SMT T 252

Note: Not all vehicles operated concurrently.

Copyright Images

The author and publisher would like to thank the following people/organisations for permission to use copyright images in this book: Peter Bradley, Michael Dryhurst, Mike Harris, Laurie James, Kevin Lane, Barry LeJeune, Gerald Mead, The Omnibus Society, Stephen Telling, Mark Worley, Tony Wright.

Every attempt has been made to seek permission for other images used in this book. However, if we have inadvertently used copyright images without permission/acknowledgement we apologise and we will make the necessary correction at the first opportunity.

Bibliography

Turns, Keith, *The Independent Bus* (Newton Abbot: David & Charles, 1974)
Wallis, Philip, *London Transport Connections 1945 – 1985* (Harrow Weald: Capital Transport Publishing, 2003)
The Little Red Book (Shepperton: Ian Allan Ltd, various dates)
Buses Illustrated, Buses (Shepperton, Addlestone: Ian Allan Ltd, Ian Allan Publishing, various dates)
The London Bus (London: London Omnibus Traction Society, various dates)
South Wales & West Branch Bulletin (Chippenham: The Omnibus Society, various dates)
News Sheets (London: The PSV Circle, various dates)
www.buslistsontheweb.co.uk